# THIS BOOK BELONG TO

________________________

________________________

________________________

# Color Test Page

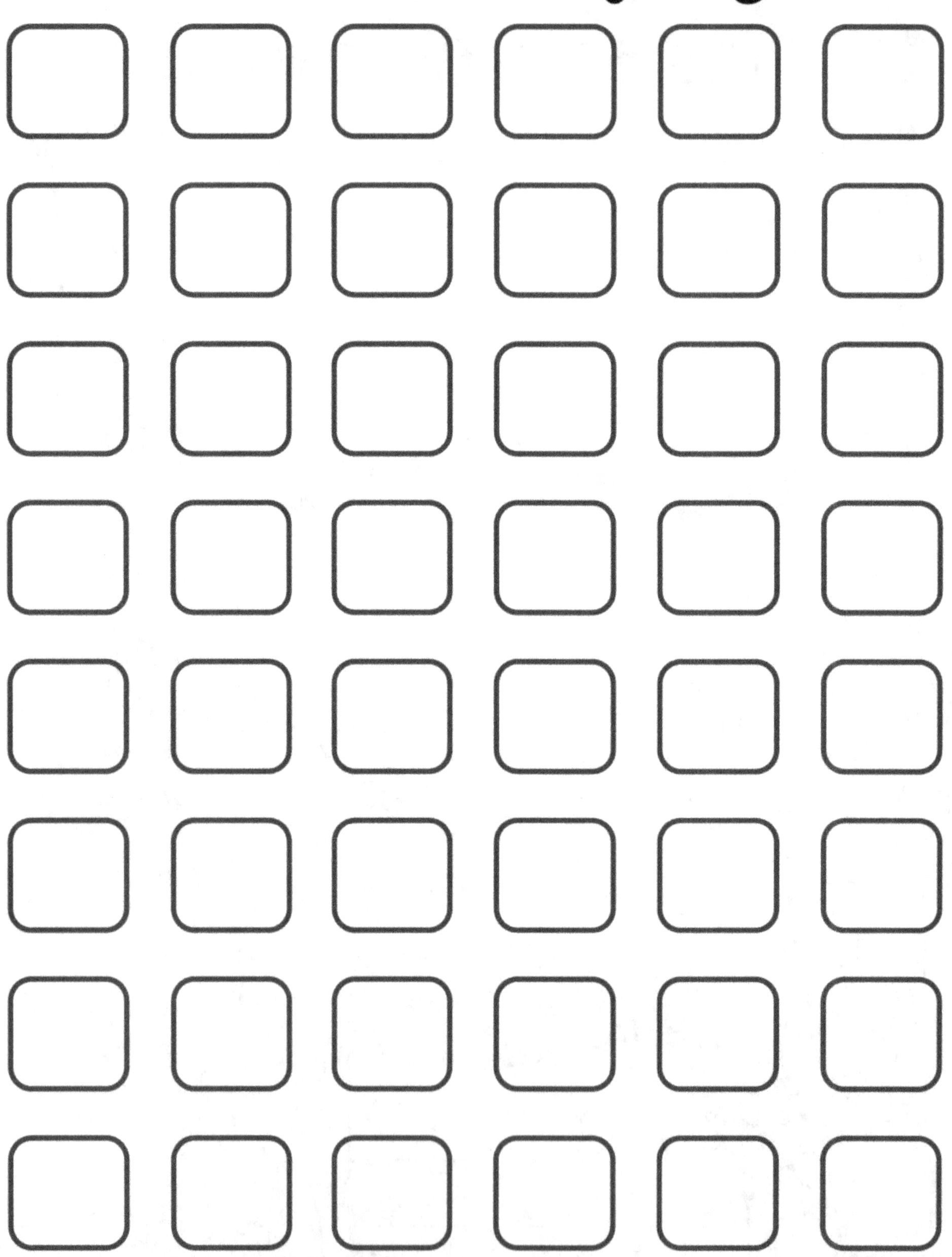

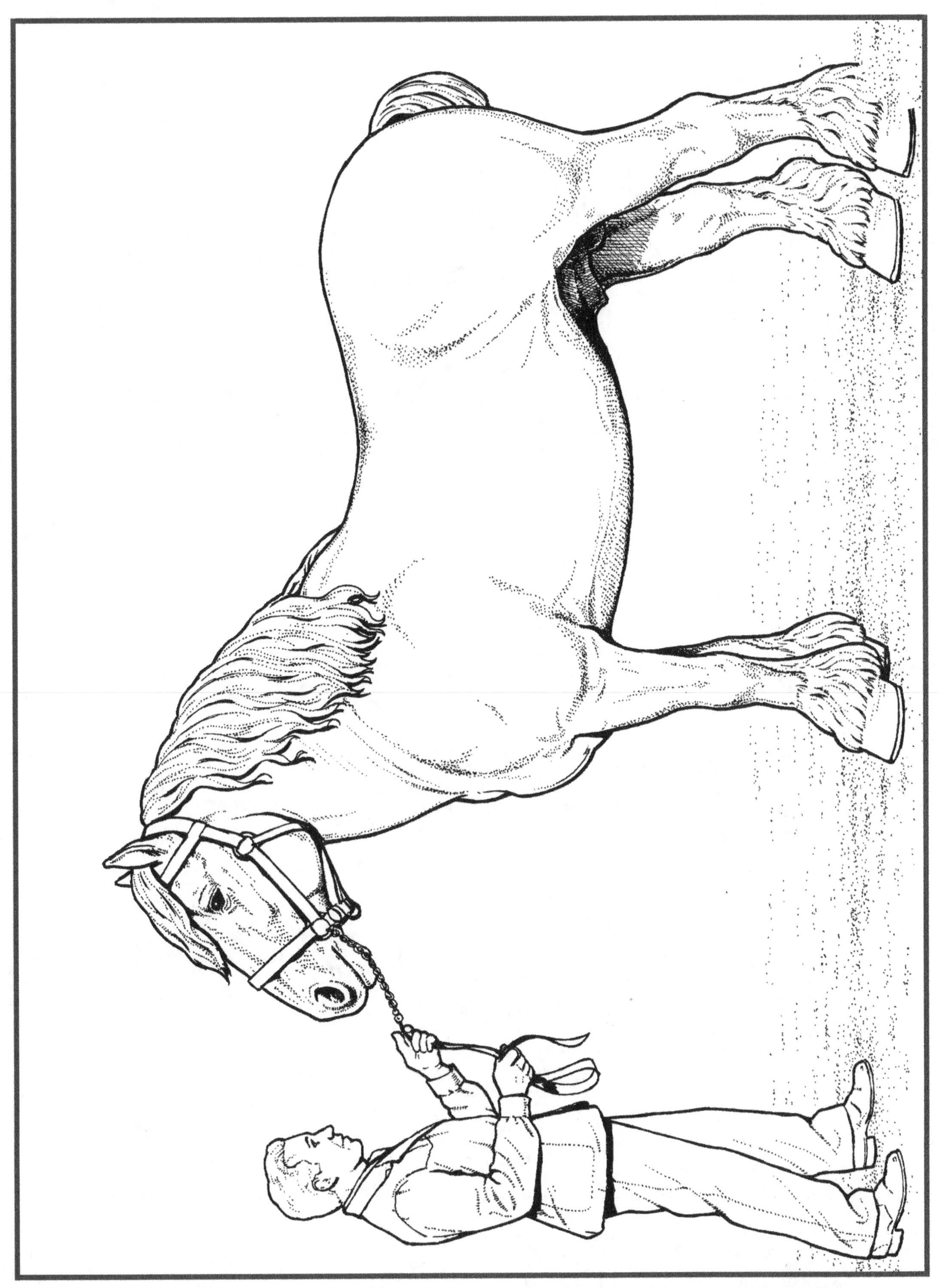

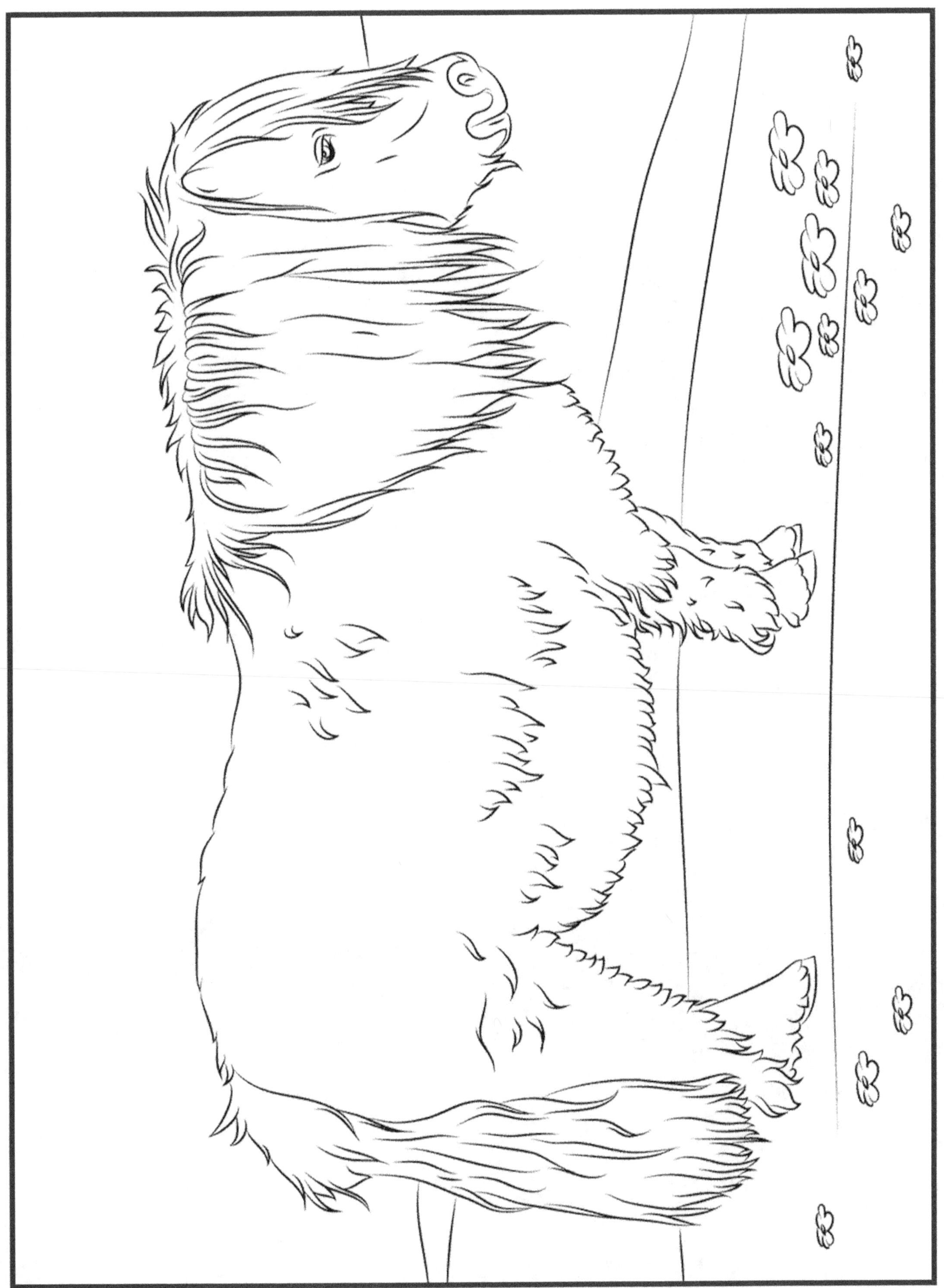

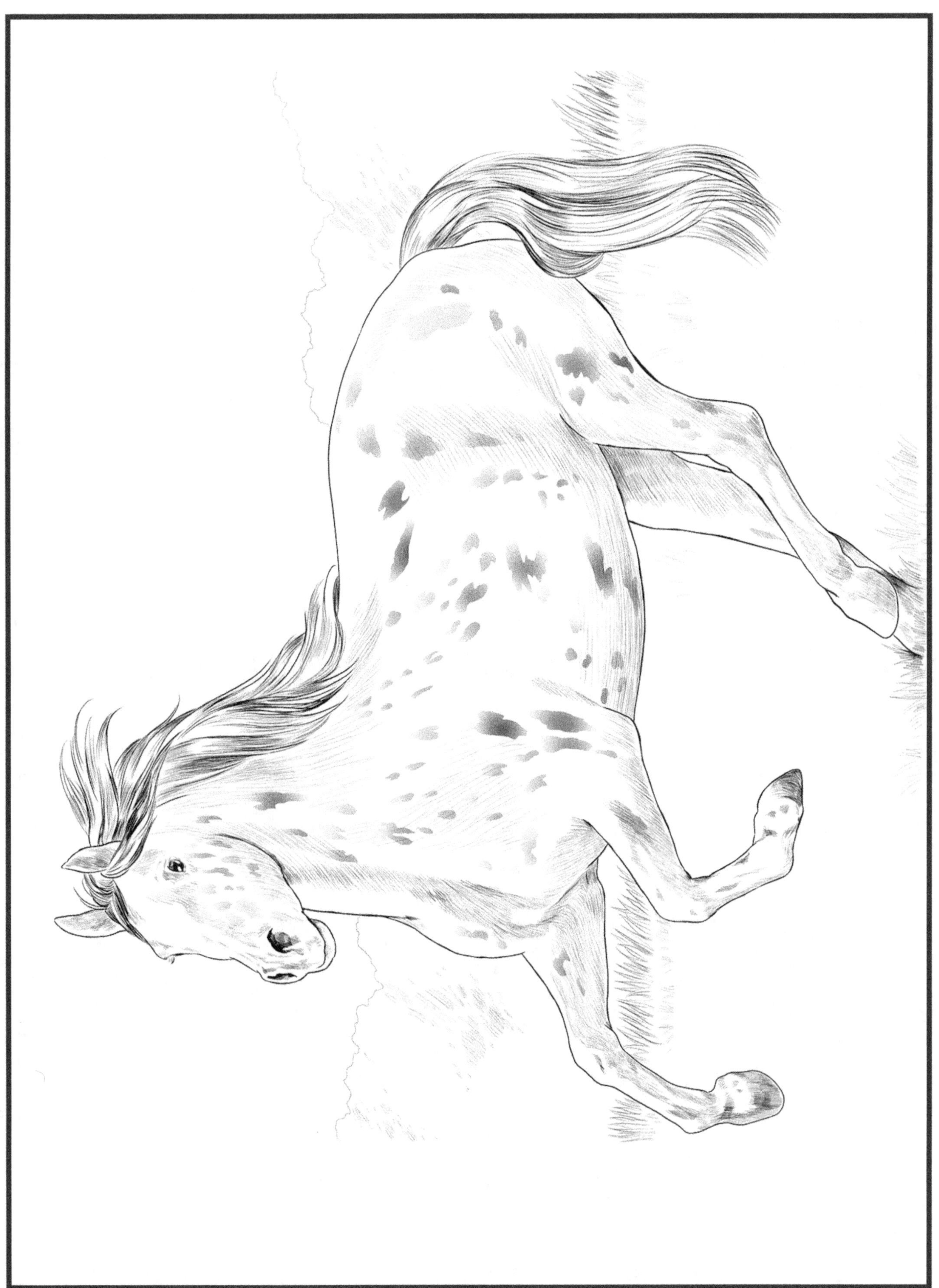

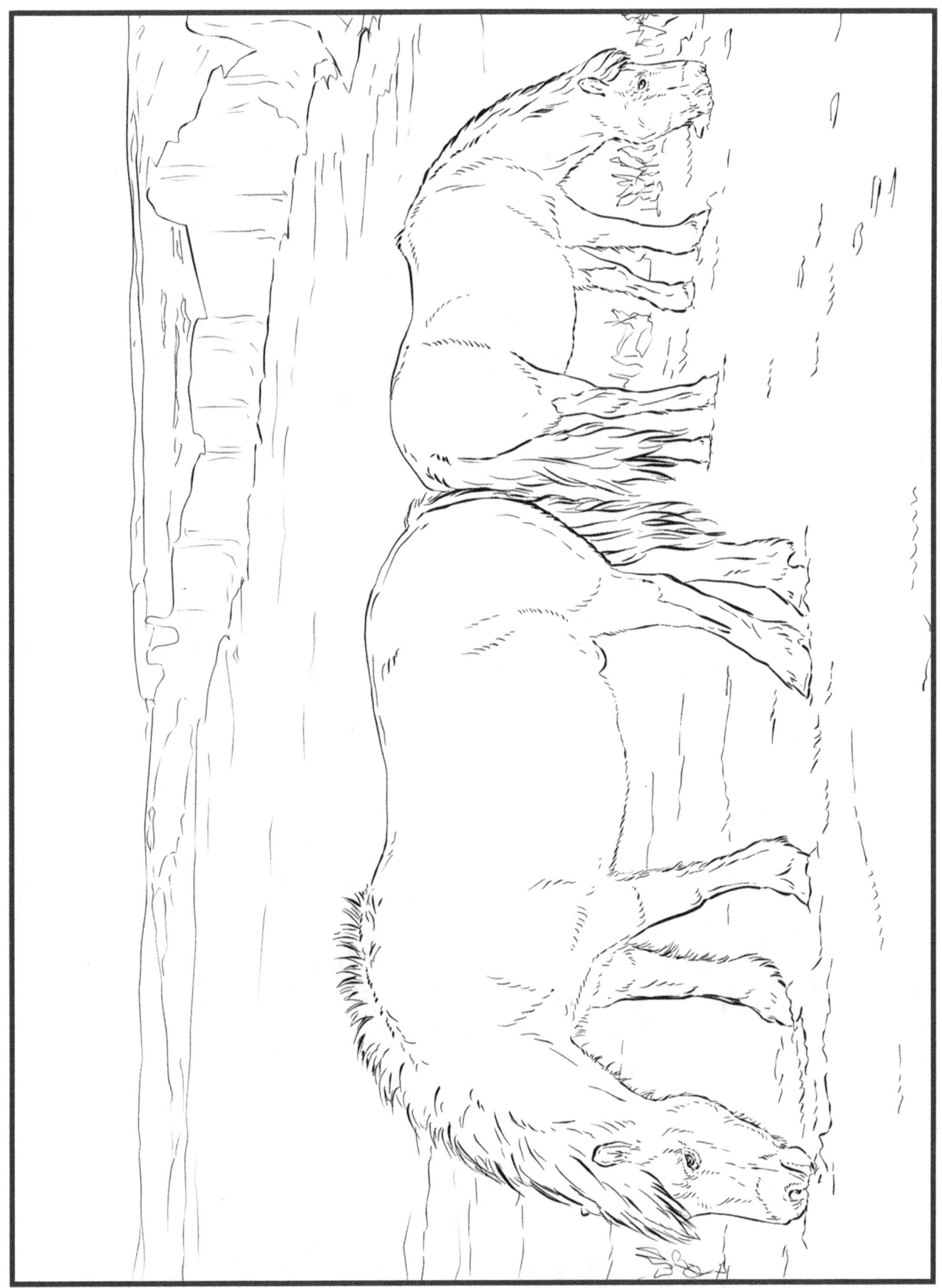

www.ingramcontent.com/pod-product-compliance
Lightning Source LLC
Chambersburg PA
CBHW081447250726
48662CB00009B/2983